HYBRID AND ELECTRIC CARS

by Rebecca Pettiford

pogo

Ideas for Parents and Teachers

Pogo Books let children practice reading informational text while introducing them to nonfiction features such as headings, labels, sidebars, maps, and diagrams, as well as a table of contents, glossary, and index.

Carefully leveled text with a strong photo match offers early fluent readers the support they need to succeed.

Before Reading

- "Walk" through the book and point out the various nonfiction features. Ask the student what purpose each feature serves.
- Look at the glossary together. Read and discuss the words.

Read the Book

- Have the child read the book independently.
- Invite him or her to list questions that arise from reading.

After Reading

- Discuss the child's questions. Talk about how he or she might find answers to those questions.
- Prompt the child to think more. Ask: Have you ever ridden in a hybrid car? How about an electric car? Did you notice ways it was different from other cars?

Pogo Books are published by Jump!
5357 Penn Avenue South
Minneapolis, MN 55419
www.jumplibrary.com

Copyright © 2017 Jump!
International copyright reserved in all countries.
No part of this book may be reproduced in any form without written permission from the publisher.

Library of Congress Cataloging-in-Publication Data

Names: Pettiford, Rebecca, author.
Title: Hybrid and electric cars / by Rebecca Pettiford.
Description: Minneapolis, MN: Jump!, Inc., [2016]
Series: Green planet | Audience: Ages 7-10.
Identifiers: LCCN 2016014974 (print)
LCCN 2016016185 (ebook)
ISBN 9781620314029 (hardcover: alk. paper)
ISBN 9781624964497 (ebook)
Subjects: LCSH: Hybrid electric cars–Juvenile literature.
Electric automobiles–Juvenile literature.
Green technology–Juvenile literature.
Classification: LCC TL221.15 .P48 2016 (print)
LCC TL221.15 (ebook) | DDC 629.22/93–dc23
LC record available at https://lccn.loc.gov/2016014974

Series Editor: Jenny Fretland VanVoorst
Series Designer: Anna Peterson
Book Designer: Leah Sanders
Photo Researcher: Kirsten Chang

Photo Credits: Alamy, 16-17, 18-19; d13/Shutterstock.com, 23; Getty, cover, 3, 5, 6-7, 12-13; J. Lekavicius/Shutterstock.com, 1; Joel_420/Shutterstock.com, 15; Paul Stringer/Shutterstock.com, 9; Shutterstock, 4, 8, 20-21; Superstock, 14; Teddy Leung/Shutterstock.com, 10-11.

Printed in the United States of America at Corporate Graphics in North Mankato, Minnesota.

TABLE OF CONTENTS

CHAPTER 1

· ·

DRIVING GREEN

Most cars on the road today run on gas. Gas is made from oil and other **fossil fuels**.

It is a **non-renewable resource**. Once it runs out, there will not be any left. We have to use gas with care.

Gas-powered cars give off **greenhouse gases**. They are bad for the **environment**.

We can drive eco-friendly or green cars. They are better for the environment. Green cars run on a combination of **electricity** and gas. Some run only on electricity.

ELECTRIC

CHAPTER 2

POWER OF TWO: HYBRID CARS

A **hybrid car** has two kinds of power. It has an **engine** that runs on gas.

It has a **motor** that runs on electricity. The two power sources work together to make a more **efficient** vehicle.

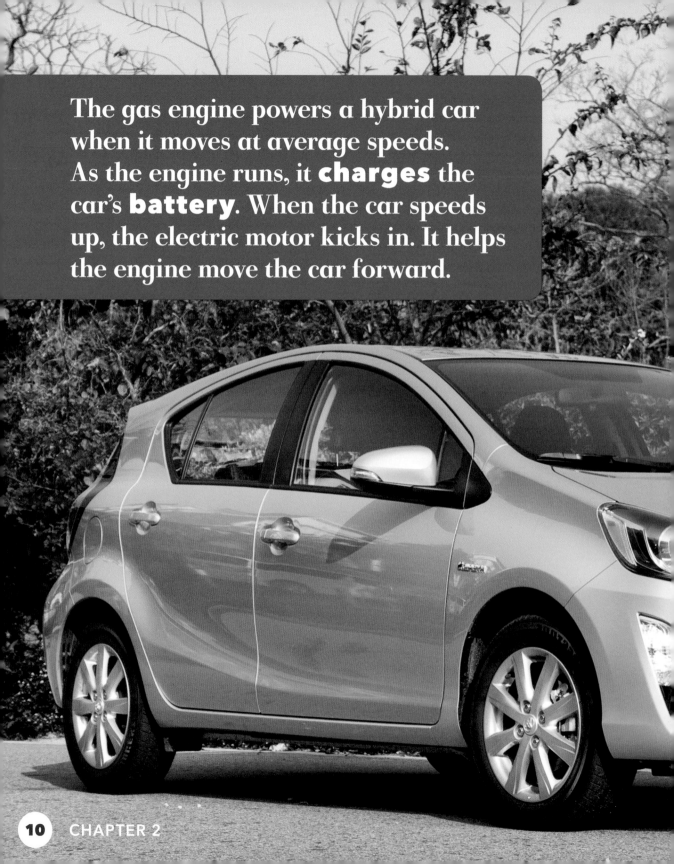

The gas engine powers a hybrid car when it moves at average speeds. As the engine runs, it **charges** the car's **battery**. When the car speeds up, the electric motor kicks in. It helps the engine move the car forward.

TAKE A LOOK!

A hybrid car uses three elements to improve efficiency.

ELECTRIC MOTOR ↔ **GAS ENGINE** ↔ **BATTERY**

Most hybrid cars still mainly run on gas. But the electric motor lets them use less of it. And less gas means fewer nasty **emissions**!

DISPLAY

INFO

CLIMATE

AUDIO

Energy monitor

OUTSIDE TEMP 13 ℃

Engine

Battery

Elec. motor

Consumption Current 0.0 MPG

10:23

CHAPTER 3

. . . .

NO GAS: ELECTRIC CARS

An **electric car** runs on electricity. Would you be surprised to learn that a third of all early cars were electric? When gas became plentiful, they disappeared.

Today people are looking for ways to use less gas. Electric cars are back!

In an electric car, the electricity is stored in a battery pack. The battery powers a motor, which turns the wheels. What happens when the electricity is used up? The driver plugs the car in to charge the battery.

TAKE A LOOK!

Unlike a hybrid car, an electric car relies entirely on electricity—no gasoline needed!

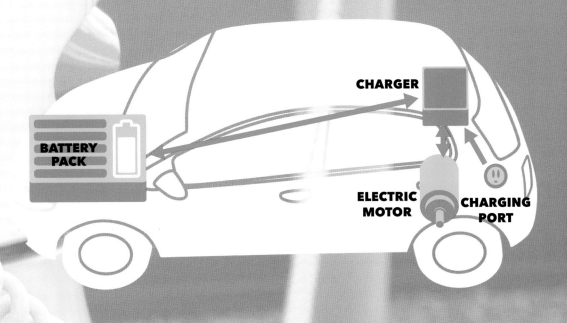

CHARGER

BATTERY PACK

ELECTRIC MOTOR

CHARGING PORT

Electric cars are quiet because they do not have engines. They save money on fuel. Drivers only pay to charge the battery. But they can only go as far as the charge will take them. Drivers must be close to charging stations.

Some drivers worry about running out of power. For them, a hybrid is a good choice. But electric cars do not use gas. They are better for the environment.

Of course, what is the "greenest" way to get somewhere? Walk, bike or take the bus!

ACTIVITIES & TOOLS

TRY THIS!

MAKE YOUR FAMILY CAR GREENER

What can you do to make your family car greener? Try these things:

1. **Keep the correct tire pressure.** This helps the car use gas efficiently. It helps tires last longer.

2. **Drive responsibly.** Speeding and slamming on the brakes wastes gas.

3. **Change the oil.** Changing the oil regularly helps the engine run better. It saves gas.

4. **Plan tune-ups.** A car that is kept in good working order uses less gas. It gives off fewer greenhouse gases.

5. **Combine short trips.** Take care of several tasks in one trip. This puts less stress on the car and helps conserve gas.

6. **Lighten up.** Do not load up the car with unnecessary items. A heavy car uses more gas.

7. **Stay cool.** When it's hot, park in the shade or in a covered garage. When the car is cool, less gas evaporates.

GLOSSARY

battery: A rechargeable device that supplies electric power to a car.

charge: To put electricity into a battery so that a machine will run.

efficient: Able to do its job with little waste.

electric car: A car that runs on electricity supplied in a battery pack.

electricity: Energy that happens in nature (as in lightning) or is made (as with a generator).

emissions: Gases given off in the process of burning fuel for energy.

engine: In a car, a machine that changes the heat from burning gas into movement or motion.

environment: The surroundings or conditions in which a person, animal, or plant lives.

fossil fuels: Fuels such as oil and natural gas that come from the dead plants and animals that have been trapped in the ground for millions of years.

greenhouse gases: Gases that are released into the air and warm Earth's surface.

hybrid car: A car that runs on both gas and electricity.

motor: A machine that runs on electricity.

non-renewable resource: A useful supply of something that cannot be easily replaced at the level at which it is used.

INDEX

TO LEARN MORE

Learning more is as easy as 1, 2, 3.

1) Go to www.factsurfer.com

2) Enter "hybridandelectriccars" into the search box.

3) Click the "Surf" button to see a list of websites.

With factsurfer, finding more information is just a click away.